R

There was
whose knol
So to save
he put it in
and instead of coming, he went.

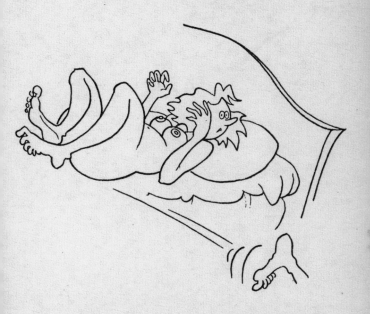

At last! A collection of Michael Rosen's _Rude Rhymes_, _Dirty Ditties_ and _Vulgar Verses_ in one unabashed dose of rudeness . . .

RUDE RHYMES

COLLECTED BY MICHAEL ROSEN
ILLUSTRATED BY RIANA DUNCAN

A SIGNET BOOK

SIGNET

Published by the Penguin Group
Penguin Books Ltd, 27 Wrights Lane, London w8 5tz, England
Penguin Books USA Inc., 375 Hudson Street, New York, New York 10014, USA
Penguin Books Australia Ltd, Ringwood, Victoria, Australia
Penguin Books Canada Ltd, 10 Alcorn Avenue, Toronto, Ontario, Canada m4v 3b2
Penguin Books (NZ) Ltd, 182–190 Wairau Road, Auckland 10, New Zealand

Penguin Books Ltd, Registered Offices: Harmondsworth, Middlesex, England

Rude Rhymes first published by André Deutsch 1989
Dirty Ditties first published by André Deutsch 1990
Vulgar Verses first published by André Deutsch 1991
First published under the title *Rude Rhymes* in one volume by Signet 1992
1 3 5 7 9 10 8 6 4 2

Typeset by DatIX International Limited, Bungay, Suffolk
Printed in England by Clays Ltd, St Ives plc

Contents

Introduction

When I was eight years old I carefully tore off the margins of several pages of the newspaper, stuck them end to end and then wrote on the long strip that I had made all the rude words I knew. I would then pull the strip between my fingers reciting the words at the top of my voice. This book is really only more of the same.

It started off on camping holidays in Wales in the fifties. Then, gathering size, first in the offices of BBC Television's *Playschool*, and then in schools where I was, in theory, supposed to be helping children write poetry. Later I started having and collecting children of my own and they have all turned into very hard-working researchers of filth.

All this produced *Rude Rhymes* (1989). It was enthusiastically received. In fact, my friends' daughter (hallo Annie) learnt to read with it. Perhaps it should become a school reader. Perhaps not.

Optimistically, I called for contributions from readers and the hundreds of offerings that came in (and are still coming in) produced *Dirty Ditties* (1990) and *Vulgar Verses* (1991). What you have in your hand (at least I assume it's what's there) is a complete edition of all three volumes.

I would love to know how to say things about this book that were both interesting and funny but I have discovered that the moment I start talking about the rhymes people yawn. They just aren't interested in me gassing on about the symbolism of squashed balls and the role of the fart in the 21st century.

May this book bring you much pleasure, no doubt not as much as the acts and organs that appear in the book but, like them, I think you will find that it can lead to many hours of fun both alone and with others.

If you think you know of songs, rhymes, riddles, definitions, puns, one-liners or any other rudeness that I've missed out, then please scribble it down and send it straight away to Michael Rosen, *Rude Rhymes*, Signet Books, 27 Wrights Lane, London w8 5TZ. Say how you would like to be mentioned, if at all, and so long as you're sure it won't bring shame on you and your family, you will get a free copy of the next book.

Sung

The white cat piddled in the black cat's eye
and the black cat said 'Gor Blimey!
I wouldn't have piddled in the white cat's eye
if I knew she was behind me.'

woman, 38
Northern Ireland

Arsehole,
arsehole,
a soldier I shall be,
to piss,
to piss,
two pistols on my knee,
fuck you,
fuck you,
for curiosity,
I'll fight for the old cunt
fight for the old cunt,
fight for the old country.

Richard Griffiths, 25, Beeston, Notts
girl, 12, Cambridgeshire

Rice an' peas an' ackee,
stick it up your battee,
mix it roun' with gravy,
an' feed it to the bald head baby.

girl, 12
London

Sung

Miss Nancy have a baby.
She call it Tiny Tim.
She put it in the bath-tub
to see if it can swim.
It dive to the bottom
it dive to the top.
Miss Nancy get excited
and grab him by his
i-tiddly-i-tee
i-tiddly-i-tee . . .

boy, 9
London

Sung

In
the
South
of
France
where the naked ladies dance
singing:
'Milly, put your willy, next to mine . . .'

girl, 13
London

Down in the valley where the grass grows green,
the white cat sat on the sewing machine.
The sewing machine went so fast,
it put ten stitches in the white cat's arse.

woman, 38
Northern Ireland

I'm not a pleasant pheasant plucker
I'm a pleasant pheasant plucker's son
and I'll go out plucking pleasant pheasants
till my pleasant pheasant plucking days are done.

Anne, 40; Eileen, 42; Jean, 30
Edinburgh

Sung

Auntie Mary had a canary
up the leg of her drawers.
When she farted
it departed
to a round of applause.

man, 22
Hertfordshire

Not last night, but the night before
three little monkeys came to the door.
One had a fiddle
one had a drum
one had pancake stuck to his bum.

Anne, 40; Eileen, 42; Jean, 30
Edinburgh

Sung

I had the German measles,
I had them very bad,
They wrapped me in a blanket,
And put me in a van.
The van was very bumpy,
And I nearly tumbled out,
And when I got to hospital,
I heard a baby shout:
'Mama, Dadda, take me home,
From this little rusty home,
I've been here for a week or two
And Oh I want to stay with you.'
Here comes Doctor Glannister,
Sliding on a banister
Half-way down he ripped his pants,
And now he's doing a cha-cha dance.

girl, 9
Northern Ireland

I was walking down the lane,
when I felt a little pain,
diarrhoea
diarrhoea.

People think it's funny,
but it's really very runny,
diarrhoea
diarrhoea.

I sat down on a chair,
and it squirted everywhere,
diarrhoea
diarrhoea.

I sat down at school,
and it squirted on the wall,
diarrhoea
diarrhoea.

I went to the headmaster,
and it came out even faster,
diarrhoea
diarrhoea.

I went to the doctors,
but now I haven't got diarrhoea
but the doctor's feeling queer
diarrhoea
diarrhoea.

girl, 7
London

Sung

In the German nick
where they hang you by the prick
and they pin dirty pictures on the walls
your mind goes blank
and you're dying for a wank
and the mice play ping pong with your balls.

boys, 12
London

Sung

I went to a Chinese restaurant
to buy a loaf of bread, bread, bread.
They wrapped it up in a five pound note
and this is what they said, said, said:

My name is Diana Dors
I'm a movie star,
I've got cute, cute tits
and a see-through bra.
I've got the lips, lips, lips,
I've got the hips, hips, hips;
turn around
movie star-ah-ah.

girls, 7
London

Sung

My boyfriend gave me an apple,
my boyfriend gave me a pear,
my boyfriend gave me a kiss on the lips
and threw me down the stairs.

I gave him back his apple,
I gave him back his pear,
I gave him back his kiss on the lips
and I threw him down the stairs.

He took me to the pictures,
to see a sexy film,
and when I wasn't looking
he kissed another girl.

I threw him over Italy,
I threw him over France.
I threw him over Germany
and he landed on his arse.

girls, 7
London

Sung

Honey you can't love two,
Honey you can't love two.
You can't love two
and still be true.
Honey you can't love two.
Lie down
oh boy
gee whizz.

Honey you can't love three,
Honey you can't love three.
You can't love three
and still love me.
Honey you can't love three.
Lie down
oh boy
gee whizz.

Honey you can't love four,
Honey you can't love four.
You can't love four
and still want more.
Honey you can't love four.
Lie down
oh boy
gee whizz.

Honey you can't love five,
Honey you can't love five.
You can't love five
and still be alive.
Honey you can't love five.
Lie down
oh boy
gee whizz.

Honey you can't love six,
Honey you can't love six.
You can't love six
and play tricks.
Honey you can't love six.
Lie down
oh boy
gee whizz.

Honey you can't love seven,
Honey you can't love seven.
You can't love seven
and still go to heaven.
Honey you can't love seven.
Lie down
oh boy
gee whizz.

Honey you can't love eight,
Honey you can't love eight.
You can't love eight
and still play straight.
Honey you can't love eight.
Lie down
oh boy
gee whizz.

Honey you can't love nine,
Honey you can't love nine.
You can't love nine
and still be mine.
Honey you can't love nine.
Lie down
oh boy
gee whizz.

girl, 11
London

Down in the valley
where nobody goes
there's a big fat lady
without no clothes.

Down comes a cowboy
clippety clop
down with his trousers
and out with his cock.

Two months later
all was well
five months later
her belly did swell.

Nine months later
her belly went pop
out came the baby
with a paralysed cock.

Ladies and gentlemen
that's not all.
The poor little bugger
only had one ball.

girl, 13
London

Sung

Down by the river
where nobody goes,
there's a Margaret Thatcher
picking her nose,
with a pick pick here
and a pick pick there
that's how Margaret picks her nose.

girls, 7
London

Chanted

One plus one,
my story's just begun
in the bedroom –
de ler-der, de ler-der
de lerdle erdle er-der.

Two plus two,
I'm telling it to you
in the bedroom –
de ler-der, de ler-der
de lerdle erdle er-der.

Three plus three,
he sat me on my knee
in the bedroom –
de ler-der, de ler-der
de lerdle erdle er-der.

Four plus four,
he got me on the floor
in the bedroom –
de ler-der, de ler-der
de lerdle erdle er-der.

Five plus five,
my legs are open wide
in the bedroom –
de ler-der, de ler-der
de lerdle erdle er-der.

Six plus six,
he's sucking at my tits
in the bedroom –
de ler-der, de ler-der
de lerdle erdle er-der.

Seven plus seven,
I think I'm up in heaven
in the bedroom –
de ler-der, de ler-der
de lerdle erdle er-der.

Eight plus eight,
the doctor's at the gate
in the bedroom –
de ler-der, de ler-der
de lerdle erdle er-der.

Nine plus nine,
the twins are doing fine
in the bedroom –
de ler-der, de ler-der
de lerdle erdle er-der.

Ten plus ten,
we're starting it again
in the bedroom –
de ler-der, de ler-der
de lerdle erdle er-der.

girl, 9
London

Tune: 'My Bonny Lies over the Ocean'

My father's a lavatory cleaner
he cleans them by day and by night
and when he comes home of an evening
his shoes are all covered in . . .

shine up your buttons with Brasso
it's only thre'pence a tin.
You can buy it or nick it from Woolies
but I doubt they've got any in.

Some say he died of the fever
some say he died of the flu
but you and I know what he died of
he died of the smell of the . . .

shine up your buttons with Brasso
it's only thre'pence a tin.
You can buy it or nick it from Woolies
but I doubt they've got any in.

Some say he's buried in a graveyard
some say he's buried in a pit.
But you and I know what he's buried in.
He's buried in six foot of . . .

shine up your buttons with Brasso
it's only thre'pence a tin.
You can buy it or nick it from Woolies
but I doubt they've got any in.

Jamie Butler, 26
Merseyside

Tune: 'Sam Hall'

There was a man called Hunt in Waterloo,
There was a man called Hunt in Waterloo,
There was a man called Hunt
who thought he had a cunt,
but his arse was on his front
in Waterloo.

There was a man called Nest in Waterloo,
There was a man called Nest in Waterloo,
There was a man called Nest
who thought he had two breasts,
but his bum was on his chest
in Waterloo.

boy, 11
London

Tune: 'Yellow Rose of Texas'

There is a winding passage
that leads up to my heart,
and what comes down this passage
is commonly called a fart.
The fart is very useful
it sets the mind at ease.
It warms the bed on wintry nights
and disinfects the fleas.

man, 42
Middlesex

When I was a wee wee tot,
they took me from my wee wee cot,
they put me on my wee wee pot
to see if I would wee or not.

When they found that I would not,
they took me from my wee wee pot.
They put me in my wee wee cot
where I wee wee quite a lot.

girl, 13
London

Tune: 'Conga'

In 1984
the monkeys had a war
they lost their guns
and used their bums
in 1984.

In 1986
the queen pulled down her nicks
she licked her bum
and said: 'Yum yum
it tastes like candy sticks.'

In 1987
the king went to heaven
he went so quick
he lost his dick
in 1987.

girl, 7
London

Sung

Passengers will please refrain
from urinating while the train
is standing in the station
or a s-i-i-i-iding.

woman, 65
London

Tune: 'D'ye ken John Peel?'

Oh-h cats on the rooftops, cats on the tiles
cats with the clap and cats with piles
cats with their arseholes wreathed in smiles,
as they revel in the joys of fornication.

Bill, 36
Ealing

Sung

When Suzy was a baby,
a baby Suzy was,
she went ga ga
a ga-ga-ga
a ga ga ga ga ga-ga-ga.

When Suzy was a toddler,
a toddler Suzy was,
she went scribble, scribble
scribble-scribble-scribble
scribble scribble scribble-scribble-scribble.

When Suzy was a Junior,
a Junior Suzy was,
she went Miss, Miss,
I need to go a piss,
I don't know where the toilet is.

When Suzy was a Secondary,
a Secondary Suzy was,
she went ooh ah,
I've lost my bra,
I left my knickers in my boyfriend's car.

When Suzy was a mummy,
a mummy Suzy was,
she went sh sh sh-sh-sh
sh sh sh sh sh-sh-sh. (rocking baby)

When Suzy was a granny,
a granny Suzy was,
she went knit knit knit-knit-knit
knit knit knit knit knit-knit-knit.

When Suzy was a skeleton,
a skeleton Suzy was,
she went rattle rattle rattle-rattle-rattle
rattle rattle rattle-rattle-rattle.

When Suzy was a ghost,
a ghost Suzy was,
she went oo oo oo-oo-oo,
oo oo oo oo oo-oo-oo.

When Suzy was an angel,
an angel Suzy was,
she went amen amen amen
start again.

girl, 7
London

Tune: 'Mademoiselle from Armentières'

There was an old lady of ninety two – parlez-vous.
There was an old lady of ninety two – parlez-vous.
There was an old lady of ninety two,
she done a fart but missed the loo,
inky pinky parlez-vous.

The fart went rolling down the street – parlez-vous.
The fart went rolling down the street – parlez-vous.
The fart went rolling down the street,
knocked a copper off his feet,
inky pinky parlez-vous.

The copper got out his rusty pistol – parlez-vous.
The copper got out his rusty pistol – parlez-vous.
The copper got out his rusty pistol,
he shot the fart from here to Bristol,
inky pinky parlez-vous.

Bristol City were playing at home – parlez-vous.
Bristol City were playing at home – parlez-vous.
Bristol City were playing at home,
they kicked the fart from here to Rome,
inky pinky parlez-vous.

Julius Caesar was drinking some gin – parlez-vous.
Julius Caesar was drinking some gin – parlez-vous.
Julius Caesar was drinking some gin,
he opened his mouth and the fart popped in,
inky pinky parlez-vous.

The fart went rolling down his spine – parlez-vous.
The fart went rolling down his spine – parlez-vous.
The fart went rolling down his spine,
banged his balls and made them chime,
inky pinky parlez-vous.

Now that's the end of my little song – parlez-vous.
That's the end of my little song – parlez-vous.
That's the end of my little song,
but the fart goes rolling on,
inky pinky parlez-vous.

boy, 17
London

(Harlem, New York skipping song)

Kiss my acker-backer
my soda cracker
my B, U, T
my doodie-hole
your ma
your pa
your greasy granny
wears dirty panties
gotta big behind
like Frankenstein
gotta root-toot-toot
like a prostitute
gotta ding dong
like King Kong
gotta beat-beat
on Sesame Street.

Karol Swanson
South Queensferry, Scotland

Tune: Regimental March of
the Grenadier Guards

There was a Scots Highlander
at the Battle of Waterloo,
a wind blew up his tartan kilt
and showed his cock-a-doodle-do.
He thought it was so pretty,
he showed it to the queen.
She said, 'Don't be so dirty,
and go and wash it clean.'

woman, 46
London

Sung

You ought to see Michael make water.
He makes such a beautiful stream.
It runs for a mile and a quarter,
And you can't see poor Michael for steam.

man, 68
London

Tune: 'John Brown's Body'

She wears her silk pyjamas in the summer when it's
   hot,
she wears her winter woollies in the winter when it's
   not.
But sometimes in the springtime,
and sometimes in the fall,
she pops between the sheets
with nothing on at all.

That's the time you wanna be there,
That's the time you wanna be there,
That's the time you wanna be there,
when she pops between the sheets
with nothing on at all.

man, 68
London

Kids in the front seat cause accidents.
Accidents in the back seat cause kids.

girl, 16
North Island, New Zealand

The world is full of feather beds
and little girls with curly heads.
So really there is no excuse,
for sodomy and self-abuse.

Dr Tim Healey, 55
Barnsley

It's better to fart and stink a little
than keep it in and be a cripple.

Angela, 32, and Jason Ward, 10
Dyfed, Wales

Never kiss your lover at the garden gate,
'cos love is blind
but the neighbours ain't.

boy, 9
London

Once a king
always a king
once a knight
is enough.

John, 28, and Linda, 25, Motyka
Melbourne, Australia

Proverb

A bird in the hand . . . does it on your wrist.

boy, 17, and girl, 13
Surrey

When you get them by the balls, their hearts and
minds will follow

Good girls go to heaven, bad girls go everywhere

If you miss your period now, don't worry, better late
than never

It's the little things that show they care – but yours is
too small

Don't leave home without it – your stretchable friend

Make it easy – practise with your pencil case

Siobhan, 15, and Sara, 16,
Herts

Sex is an evil
evil is a sin.
Sin is forgivable
so get stuck in.

Adam Prout, 15
London

Watership Down
you've read the book,
you've seen the film
– now eat the pie.

boy, 17, and girl, 13
Surrey

36

Be ozone friendly –
fart in a bottle!

J. Dent, 20
Norwich

Every little bean
must be heard
as well as seen.

man, 69
London

Baked beans – good for your heart,
the more you eat – the more you fart.
The more you fart, the better you feel,
so eat baked beans for every meal.

man, 42
Middlesex

Every little helps,
as the old man said
as he pissed in the sea.

man, 68
London

If your mouth was an arsehole
and your arsehole was a mouth,
you'd be blowing shit out both ends
and yelling out your dick for help.

girl, 16
North Island, New Zealand

The higher up the mountain
the sweeter grows the grass,
the higher up the donkey climbs
the more it shows its face.

man, 68
London

A Crock of Wit

A rooster says cock-a-doodle-do.
A prostitute says, any cock'll do.

John, 28, and Linda, 25, Motyka
Melbourne, Australia

Bus Journey

Bank, St Paul's
and Elephant and Castle
Turnham Green
and Peckham Rye.

Bang your balls
on the elephant's arsehole
turn'em green
and peck'em ripe.

man, 68
London

Piccadilly Line

Is this Cockfosters?
No, it's mine.

man, 68
London

Is Mr Jones free?
No, but he's very reasonable.

man, 60
Middlesex

Advert

Use Ex-lax
to Re-lax
your bo-lax

Bryan H. Voyle, 44
Cornwall

How's your bum for lovebites?
Alright, on the whole.

Gabi Parsons, 26
Bucks

42

Dear Mr Johnson,
I am very sorry
but you will have to excuse Vicky for PE
she has diarrhoea.
It runs in the family.

girl, 13
London

A Man's Life

20–30 Tri-weekly
30–40 Try weekly
40–50 Try weakly
50–60 Beer is best

Nick the Greek, 26
London

'Children children.'
'Yes mama.'
'Where were you?'
'At grandmama's.'
'What did you eat?'
'Cheese and bread.'
'Where's my share?'
'Up in the air.'
'How shall I get it?'
'Stand on a broken chair.'
'Suppose I fall . . .?'
'I don't care.'
'Who taught you manners?'
'The dog.'
'Who's the dog?'
'YOU!'

boy, 12
London, Jamaican origin

She said: 'Would you like to kiss me?'
So he kissed her.
She said: 'Would you like to undress me?'
So he undressed her.
She said: 'Take your clothes off.'
So he took his clothes off.
She said: 'Get into bed with me.'
So he got into bed with her.
She said: 'Now do the dirtiest thing you know in the
whole wide world.'
So he got out of bed
and wrote 'BUM' on the wall.

man, 42
Middlesex

'Who do you stick up for?'
'I stick up for my mum.'
'I stick up for my dad
he stuck up for me.'

man, 60
Middlesex

'My daughter will now sing.'
'Will she, fuck!'
'One question at a time, please.'

man, 60
Middlesex

Tongue-twister

Suzy sits in the shoe-shine shop
she sits and shines
she shines and sits.

Kate Lawrie, 18, and sister, 19
Bucks

Say quickly:

I chased a bug around a tree
I'll get his blood he knows I will.

Julian Foster, 18
Beckenham, Kent

The cat crept into the crypt
crapped
and crept out again.

man, 43
London

Spell **PIG** backwards and add 'funny' to it.

John, 28, and Linda, 25, Motyka
Melbourne, Australia

Try this:

Put your fingers in the corners of your mouth,
pull out your cheeks and say, 'My dad's a banker'.

boy, 13
London

Three men were walking along when they came to a cave. One of them went in and saw a piece of toast in there. He went to pick it up when he heard this voice say:

I'M THE GHOST
THAT GUARDS THE TOAST

so the man ran out, and he says to the others,
'Don't go in there, there's a ghost in there.'
But the second man says, 'I ain't scared, I'm going in.'

So he goes in and he sees the piece of toast and he goes to pick it up when he hears the voice:

I'M THE GHOST
THAT GUARDS THE TOAST

so the man ran out and he says to the third man,
'Don't go in there, there's a ghost in there.'
But the third man says, 'I ain't scared, I'm going in.'

So he goes in and he sees the piece of toast and he thinks, I ain't bothered, and he grabbed it and stuffed it in his mouth and ate it all up. And the voice called out:

I WARNED YOU ONCE
I WARNED YOU TWICE
I WIPE MY BUM
ON EVERY SLICE.

boy, 9
London

Salvation Army

'Sister Anna will carry the banner!'
'But I carried it last week!'
'You'll carry it every bloody week!'
'But I'm in the family way!'
'You're in every bugger's way!'

man, 60
Middlesex

These two tramps were walking along the road
when they came to a pile of dog shit.
They looked at it
and one said,
It looks like it.
The other said.
It feels like it.
Then one said,
It tastes like it.
Then they stepped over it and said,
Lucky we didn't tread in it.

man, 42
Middlesex

Say 'Polish it in the corner' very quickly over and
over again.

man, 42
Middlesex

Are you coming?
No, it's just the way my trousers hang.

man, 44
London

Latin

Boyibus kissibus
sweet girliorum
girlibus likibus
wanti sumorum.

Dr Tim Healey, 55
Barnsley

Fuzzy Duck

(Game for more than four, preferably when some or all are drunk:)

Sit in a ring and first person says: 'To my left fuzzy duck' so the person on the left has to say: 'To my left fuzzy duck' and so on round the ring until someone, (anyone) says 'Does he?' then back goes the phrase but this time as 'To my right ducky fuzz'. When someone says 'Does he?' change direction again and go back to 'To my left fuzzy duck'.

Whoever says: 'Duzzy fuck' or 'Fucky duzz' pays a penalty (?!) and that person has to restart the game.

boy, 15
Strathclyde

Newspaper headline:

LADY TRUCKDRIVER SWERVES TO
AVOID CHILD
– and falls out of bed.

Dr Tim Healey, 55
Barnsley

51

It depends how you read it:

BRITISH TROOPS' PUSH
Bottles up Germans
(newspaper headline: 1944)

or

**BRITISH TROOPS
PUSH BOTTLES UP GERMANS**

Who is Sylvia? What is she?
(Elizabethan song)

or

Who is Sylvia?
What?
Is she?

man, 40-ish
Reading, Berks

Headline in US paper:

NUT SCREWS WASHER AND BOLTS

man, 43
Middx

Oh shit! said the king
and his word was law,
thirty thousand courtiers
straining on the floor.

man, 42
Middlesex

I lost my leg in the army
I lost my leg in the navy
I lost my cock in the butcher's shop
and I found it in the gravy.

Anne, 40; Eileen, 42; Jean, 30
Edinburgh

Here's to the game of twenty toes,
It's played all over the town,
The girls play it with ten toes up,
The boys with ten toes down.

David Morris
Birmingham

Batman and Robin were in Batmobile,
Batman done a fart and paralysed the wheel.
The brakes couldn't take it
the engine fell apart,
all because of Batman and his supersonic fart.

boy, 11
London

I kissed her lips
while making passes,
She closed her legs
and broke my glasses

girl, 14
London

A sigh is but a puff of wind
coming from the heart,
if it should take a downward course
it's often called a fart.

To fart it gives you pleasure
it gives the bowels ease.
It warms and airs the blankets
and drives away the fleas.

Mrs A. Smith, 40
Surrey

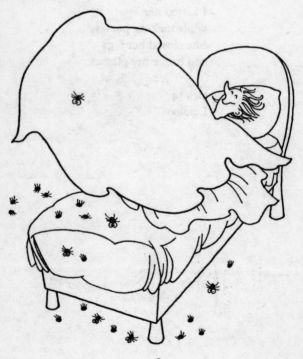

58

My friend Billy's got a ten foot willy,
he showed it to the girl next door.
She thought it was a snake
so she hit it with a rake,
and now it's only four foot four.

woman, 38
Northern Ireland

There was an old fakir of India
who thought of a wonderful trick,
he greased his arsehole with butter
and slowly inserted his prick.
It wasn't for fame or fortune
or any fabulous wealth.
It was just to please an old comrade
who told him to fuck himself.

man, 70
London

Molly owned a shellfish stall
She'd serve you in a twinkle
And if you didn't know the way,
She'd soon fish out your winkle.

Barry Saunders, 31
Herts

The doggies held a conference
they came from near and far.
Some of them came by aeroplane
and some by motor car.

As each doggy queued
to see the visitors' book,
each doggy took its arsehole off
and hung it on a hook.

As they were assembled
each pure breed dam and sire,
some dirty rotten bastard
came in and shouted, 'FIRE!'

The dogs were in a panic,
they had no time to look,
so each dog grabbed an arsehole
off the nearest hook.

And that is why you'll see today
a dog will leave a bone
to sniff another's arsehole
to see if it's their own.

Gareth Jackson, 14
Stockport

Titsaleena Bumsquirt Big Banana Feet
went to the pictures and fell through the seat.
When the picture started
Titsaleena farted
Titsaleena Bumsquirt Big Banana Feet.

Ian Hodgkinson, 14
Arizona, USA

I wish I were a caterpillar
for life would be a farce.
I'd climb up all the buds and trees
and slide down on my . . . hands and knees.

Dr Tim Healey, 55
Barnsley

Do not blame poor doggy,
it's not his fault at all.
Someone left a wet umbrella
hanging in the hall.

Dr Tim Healey, 55
Barnsley

As I was walking down the town
I saw two people lying down.
Her skirt was up,
his arse was bare
I saw the flesh beneath the hair.
His balls they twangled to and fro
if that's not fucking, I don't know.

Anne, 40; Eileen, 42; Jean, 30
Edinburgh

Fatty and Skinny were in the bath
Fatty farted and Skinny laughed.

Kate Angel, 21
London

Fatty and Skinny went to the zoo
Skinny got stuck in some elephant's poo.

Michael Rockwell, 19
Inverness

Fatty and Skinny went up in a rocket,
Fatty came down with shit in his pocket.

Fatty and Skinny in bed,
Fatty rolled over and Skinny was dead.

boy, 7
London

How do you do it?
Putting on a 'Joe'.
It takes me an hour to put it on
and all she wants is a blow.

girl, 16
North Island, New Zealand

When you get married
and you have twins,
don't come to me
for safety pins.

Ghisleine Quinn, 15
Stockport

Creepy crawly custard
green snot pie,
all mashed up with a dead dog's eye.
Slugs and bogies spread on thick
all washed down
with a cup of cold sick.

girl, 13
London

Dan, Dan the sanitary man
Superintendent-General of the lavatory pan.
He puts in the paper
and changes the towels
works to the rhythm of the rumbling bowels.

Carolyn Skudder, 30
Devon

I'm not dumb,
I'm not silly,
I hang on
to Daddy's willy.

boy, 11
London

Um Chukka Willy
of Coconut Grove
was a mean motherfucker
you could tell by his clothes.
Black leather jacket
and hairy arse,
between his balls was a patch of grass,
led a hundred women
through a hole in the wall,
swore to the devil
he'd fuck'em all.
At ninety nine
he had to stop,
the friction on his balls
was about to pop.
Went to the doctor
and the doctor said,
'Um Chukka Willy
your balls are dead.'

boy, 11
London

Big Ben
strikes ten
does a fart
now and then.

boy, 7
London

Little winkles in their shells,
I think it is a sin,
to pick the little buggers out
and eat them off a pin.

woman, 25
London

My name's Ben
and I live in a tree,
sell condoms
for 25p.
I would sell them
for half a bob,
but that all depends
on the size of your knob.

boy, 11
London

My big mum
has a very big bum
and a very big bum has she.
She sits in the dark
in the middle of the park
scratching her bum like me.

boy, 11
London

I went into a treacle shop
to buy half a pound a treacle
and who do you think I met?
Mickey Thumb.
He asked me if I'd go to the fair,
and I thought a bit
and I thought a bit
and I said I didn't mind.
And it were a fair.

So I come home
and took me bonnet off
and a knock came at the door
and who do you think that was?
Mickey Thumb's uncle
to say that he were ill
and would I go and visit him.
So I thought a bit
and I thought a bit
and I said I didn't mind.
And he were ill.

I came in
took me bonnet off
and a knock came at the door
and who do you think that was?
Mickey Thumb's father
to say that he were dead
and would I go to the funeral.
So I thought a bit
and I thought a bit
and I said I didn't mind.
And it were a funeral.

Some laughed over his grave
Some cried over his grave
but I spat over his grave
in 'membrance of Mickey Thumb.

girl, 12, London
learnt from mother (Manchester)

If all the boys lived over the sea
what a great swimmer Mary would be.

If all the boys ate greasy chips
wouldn't Mary have greasy lips?

Kate Lawrie, 18, and sister, 19
Bucks

Hunch Bunch, call the Judge,
Mother's having a baby.
Is it a boy?
Is it a girl?
Is it a human baby?

Wrap it up in tissue paper.
Throw it down the escalator.
First floor – drop.
Second floor – drop.
Third floor – kick the door.
Mother's not having a baby no more.

girl, 12
London

Pick it
lick it
roll it
flick it

man, 43
Middlesex

He took me to the pictures
to get me dolly mixtures
and every time the light went out
he looked right up my knickers.

girl, 12
London

Tarzan swings
Tarzan falls
Tarzan hurts
his hairy balls.

Siobhan, 15, and Sara, 16
Herts

What's the time?
Half past nine,
hang your knickers on the line.

When a copper
comes along,
take them off
and put them on.

man, 42
Middlesex

Where have you gone, Willy, Willy?
Up the town, Willy, Willy.
Where's your money, Willy, Willy?
In my pocket, Willy, Willy.
Let me feel, Willy, Willy.
Feel your own, Willy, Willy.

boy, 9
Scotland

Three nudes in a fountain,
Along comes handsome Errol Flynn.
Out comes his hairy monster
Which one will he stuff it in?

Make it mine, make it mine, make it mine.

girl, 13
London

Oh where is my smoky
all covered in sand?
I killed a Leeds United supporter
with an elastic band.

I went to his funeral
I went to his grave
the vicar came up to me
and asked me my name.
I answered politely
with a bicycle chain.

He took me to court for this
and the judge so did say,
'You will go to Borstal
for a year and one day.'

Me old woman fainted
me old man dropped dead,
and me poor little brother
shot the judge in the head.

There's bars on the windows
there's bars on the door
and even the piss pot
is chained to the floor.

boy, 12
London

Wherever you are
wherever you be
always let
your wind go free
for refraining to fart
was the death of me.

Mother-in-law,
London

You want triplets
I want twins.
Let's go to bed
and see who wins.

Ghisleine Quinn, 15
Stockport

Whoever smelt it
dealt it.

Whoever denied it
supplied it.

boy, 9
London

I went to the duchess for tea,
she said, 'Do you fart when you pee?'
I answered with wit,
'Do you pee when you shit?'
which I really thought, one up to me.

woman, 73
Norfolk

Your Bob
owes our Bob
one bob
and if your Bob
don't give our Bob
that bob
that your Bob
owes our Bob
then our Bob
will give
your Bob
a bobbin' bloomin' eye.

boy, 11
London

Now here's a simple story
as simple as can be.
The place is Piccadilly,
the players: He and She.

She says, 'Will it hurt me?'
'Of course not,' says he.
'It's just a simple process,
as simple as can be.'

He gives a sudden jerk,
she cries, 'It bloody hurts,
thank God it's all over,
thank God he's pulled it out.'

Now, if you read this carefully,
A Dentist you will find.
It's not what you were thinking,
it's just your dirty mind.

Julie Harrison, 20
Swansea, Wales

Here lies the body
of dear old Dick
who went through life
with a twisted prick.

All his life
was a lifelong hunt
looking for the girl
with the twisted cunt.

When he found one
he dropped down dead,
for the one he found
had a left-hand thread.

man, 70
London

The fart is a wonderful creature
it lives in the Valley of Bum.
It travels around in your knickers
and comes out with a musical hum.

Kate Angel, 21
London

Chant

'Balls to the baker.'
'BROWN BREAD!'

'Who fucked the baker?'
'OLD FRED!'

'Where did he do it?'
'IN BED!'

'What were his balls like?'
'ALL RED!'

'How do you know that?'
'I'M FRED!'

Nick the Greek, 26
London

What's the time? Half past nine
hang your knickers on the line.
When they're dry, bring them in,
put them in a biscuit tin.
Eat a biscuit, eat a cake,
eat your knickers by mistake.

girl, 8
Surrey

Poor old Santa, poor old guy,
by jeepers and by jiminy,
he only comes but once a year
and then it's down the chimney.

man, first heard in 1962
USA

Little Robin Redbreast
sat upon a pole,
lifted up his left leg
and whistled up his hole.

Danny, 36
Bromley, Kent

Silence in court,
The judge is dead.
Someone has farted
and blew off his head.

Kerry Connor, 11
Sennelager, Germany

Julius Caesar dropped a breezer,
his mother went to catch it.
His father hid behind the door
and hit it with a hatchet.

K. Da'Casto, 19
Newbury, Berks

A man's occupation
is to stick his cockulation
in the woman's fertilization
to make the next generation.

girl, 14
London

'Tis a man's occupation
to stick his knobulation
up a woman's ventilation
to increase the population
of the younger generation.
I got this information
from the board of education
after a detailed demonstration
by two teachers on the floor.

Karen Godliman, 13
Woking, Surrey

There was Superman flying around
when he spotted Supergirl lying on the ground.
In the nude, legs in air, he thought, 'What luck!
I'll nip down quick and give her a fuck!'

Batman grabbed him as he flew past:
'You're much too late, you stupid arse.
You'd get a shock,' he said with a grin.
'The Invisible Man's already in.'

Frank, 43
Brentford, Middx

A fairy's life is very hard,
up where the tinsel flickers.
Golden wand in one hand,
and a fir tree up her knickers.

Karen Godliman, 13
Woking, Surrey

Spider, spider
on the wall,
ain't you got no
sense at all?
Can't you see
the wall's been plastered?
Now you're stuck
you silly bastard.

Karen Godliman, 13
Woking, Surrey

'Tis dogs' delight
to bark and bite
and little birds to sing,
but when the beastly fly comes round
it shits on everything.

man, 55

Mavis had a little dog
of all she loved him most.
He lifted up his little leg
and peed against the post,
but when the post began to steam
he thought it was on fire,
so he lifted up his little leg
and peed a little higher.

girl, 13
London

Have you ever caught your dick in a mangle,
when some bloody fool turns the handle?
Your nuts go crack,
your dick flips back,
have you ever caught your dick in a mangle?

Carla Holden, 15
Cumbria

Jack McGrew was five foot two,
and hated the way he was built,
'cos dogs would follow him all around
and sniff right up his kilt.

Barry Saunders, 31
Herts

'If skirts become much shorter,'
said the typist with a blush,
'there'll be two more cheeks to powder
and a lot more hair to brush.'

Dr Tim Healey, 55
Barnsley

Little Boy Brown
went to town
riding on a donkey;

did a fart
in the cart
and made the wheels go wonky.

boy, 8
London

I had a little poodle dog
a poodle dog was he.
He lifted up his poodle leg
and poodled over me.

girl, 12
London

I love you, I love you, I love you almighty.
I wish your pyjamas were next to my nightie.
I hope you're not mistaken, I hope I haven't tricked you
I mean on the clothes line and not in the bed.

boy, 9
London

I swear to God I love you,
I love you 'cos you're good.
You're good because God made you,
by God I wish I could.

Dr Tim Healey, 55
Barnsley

My girl sucked my willy
till it turned blue,
now it's shrivelled up
and looks like a shoe.

Jack Staples, 13
South London

Long and thin, goes too far in
and does not please the ladies.
Short and thick just does the trick
and manufactures babies.

Anne, 40; Eileen, 42; Jean, 30
Edinburgh

There's a copper round the corner
eating cherry pie.
I asked him for a skinny bit
and he poked me in the eye,
I went and told me mother,
me mother wouldn't come.
I went and got a lollipop
and stuck it up his bum.

woman, 30
Birmingham

Walking in the jungle,
stick in me hand,
I'm a mean motherfucker,
I'm a condom man.
Look up in the tree,
what do I see?
Another motherfucker
trying to piss on me.

Picked up a rock,
threw it at his cock.
Oh my god!
he must have got
some helluva shock.

boy, 11
London

If you suck my tits
I'll suck your bits.

girls, 13
Isle of Wight

Oh Gor Blimey, Mother can't find me,
under the table, playing with Mabel,
up goes the petticoat, down go the drawers,
my little winkle, just fits yours.

woman, 69
Chatham

I'm a little Dutch boy,
I don't swear,
shit, bugger, arsehole,
I don't care.

Richard Griffiths, 25
from childhood, Beeston, Notts

I don't drink
I don't smoke
I don't swear
ah shit, I left my fags at the pub

Ritchie Shipton, 13
Herts

I asked, how come the wind blows?
God said, fuck knows.

girl, 13
Bucks

Apple tart makes you fart
custard powder makes it louder.

Michelle Ricketts, 10
Gwent, Wales

Down in the lavatory
ten foot deep,
there lies a sausage
fast asleep.
Do not stir him
he's at rest.
Beecham's pills
have done their best.

man, 42
Middlesex

Down in sweet Texas where the cow shit lay thick,
I lay on the grass with my hands on my prick,
waiting for the girl that I love and adore,
Sweet Mary, oh my dairy, my girl for evermore.

boy, 11
London

There was a cow stood in a field,
silly cow she wouldn't yield.
The reason why she wouldn't yield,
she didn't like her udders feeled.

Barry Saunders, 31
Herts

A sexy PT teacher had a voice both loud and rasping.
And when she'd finished with the boys
they were on their knees and gasping.

Barry Saunders, 31
Herts

Abraham Lincoln was a very good man,
he jumped out of the window with his dick in his hand.
He said, 'Excuse me, ladies, I'm just doing my duty,
now pull down your pants and gimme some booty!'

Joe Sender, 11
London

Wouldn't it, wouldn't it
wouldn't it be funny
if a lady had a wooden tit
wouldn't it be funny?

Carolyn Skudder, 30
Devon

I saw a young sailor who was sitting on a rock
was swinging and swaying his big hairy . . .

Fist, and the lady next door in the Ritz
was teaching the children to play with her . . .

Ice-creams and marbles and all things galore
along came a lady that looked like . . .

Shakespeare, and he was a man of wit
and on his shirt he had some . . .

Buttons, and while he was passing by St Paul's
a lady came up and grabbed him by the . . .

Arm, and she said you look like a man of pluck,
let's go home and have a cup of tea.

Nick the Greek, 26
London

Good morning, sergeant major
and bless your very soul
I tried to fuck your daughter
but I couldn't find the hole.

When I found the hole
beneath her frilly frock,
believe me, sergeant major
I couldn't find my cock.

When I found my cock
all slimy and thin,
believe me, sergeant major
I couldn't get it in.

When I got it in
and wriggling it all about
believe me, sergeant major
I couldn't get it out.

When I got it out
all red and sore
believe me, sergeant major
the bugger asked for more.

Nick the Greek, 26
London

Ask your mother for fifty cents
to see the lion jump the fence.
He jumped so high
he touched the sky
and didn't come back
till the 4th of July.

Ask your mother for fifty more
to see the lion swim ashore.
He swam so fast
he cut his arse
on a piece of looking-glass.

man, 68
London

Little bird flying high
drops his luggage from the sky.
Angry farmer wipes his eye
thanking god that cows don't fly.

man, 42
Middlesex

'Twas a dark and stormy night,
The lavatory was dim.
There came a crash
and then a splash.
Good god! she's fallen in.

girl, 13
London

In days of old
when knights were bold
and condoms weren't invented
they wrapped their socks
around their cocks
and babies were prevented.

Lee Dawson Geldard, 14
Bridlington, North Humberside

In days of old when knights were bold
and toilets weren't invented,
they dropped their load
in the middle of the road
and went home quite contented.

woman, 50
Holland

In days of old
when knights were bold
and women weren't invented
they drilled some holes
in telegraph poles
and had to be contented.

Gary Welsh, 24
Bristol

In days of old
when knights were bold
and people were contented,
they wiped their arse
on a piece of glass
and drove themselves demented.

man, 70
London

The boy stood on the burning deck
eating a tuppenny Walls,
a bit dropped down his trouser leg
and paralysed his balls.

The boy stood on the burning deck
playing a game of cricket,
the ball flew down his trouser leg
and hit his middle wicket.

man, 42
Middlesex

The boy stood on the burning deck
with a pocketful of crackers,
the flames shot up his trouser leg
and blew off both his knackers.

Paul Stanfield, 22
Stoke-on-Trent

The boy stood on the burning deck
the flames around him flickers.
He said, 'It doesn't bother me,
I've got asbestos knickers.'

Sheila, 17
Hampstead, London

The boy stood on the burning deck,
his lips were all a-quiver.
He gave a cough
and his cock fell off
and floated down the river.

Kate Lawrie, 18, and sister, 19
Bucks

The boy stood on the burning deck
his thing was covered in blisters.
The doctors came and cut it off
and now it's like his sister's.

Emma, 14
Dorset

The boy stood on the burning deck
and wondered why he'd been born.
His father said, 'You wouldn't have been
if the Durex hadn't torn.'

Katie, 12
Clwyd

The boy stood on the burning deck
his father called him lobbes
because he wouldn't wash his face
and go to schul on shabbes.

'lobbes' = lout
'schul' = synagogue
'shabbes' = sabbath

man, 68
London

Roses are red
violets are blue
I'm in bed
where are you?

Nicola Best, 20
Wiltshire

Roses are red
dahlias are pink
my feet are pretty
but your feet stink.

girl, 12
London

Roses are red
Violets are blue
. . . hanging on next door's line.

Dr Tim Healey, 55
Barnsley

When roses are red
they're ready for plucking
when girls are sixteen
they're ready for fucking.

boy, 10
London

It was Christmas day in the workhouse
the mould was on the walls,
the vicar was preaching to the inmates
and someone shouted, 'Balls!'

'I'll give you balls, you bastard,
you damned ungrateful sod,
I'll stop your Christmas pudding,
I'll see to that, by God.'

All was silent when Michael Rosen [or whoever]
shouted out, as bold as brass,
'We don't want your Christmas pudding,
you can stuff it up your arse.'

'Seize him,' shouted the vicar,
himself he found hard to restrain.
On this Holy order, Rosen's head went down the
    lavatory pan,
and some cunt pulled the chain.

John Bolt
Stroud, Gloucs

The owl and the pussycat went to sea
in a beautiful pea-green boat.
The pussycat's pee was greener still
and kept them both afloat.

children, 5
Hammersmith, London

Sung

My old man's a dustman
he wears a dustman's hat,
he killed two thousand Germans
so what do you think of that?

One lay here,
one lay there,
one lay round the corner.
One lay up Dusty Street
crying out for water.
Water, water, water,
water came at last,
I don't want no water
so stick it up your elbow.

boy, 12
London

Tune: 'Lavender's Blue'

Bogwater blue, willy willy,
bogwater blue.
When I have weed, willy willy,
bogwater green.

woman, 39
Herts

Tune: Cub Scouts' Song 'Woodpecker's Hole'

Oh I put my finger up a woodpecker's hole
the woodpecker said, 'God bless my soul!
keep it up
keep it up
keep it up
gor blimey.'

I stuck it up once, I stuck it up twice
the woodpecker said, 'Oh Christ, that's nice.
keep it up
keep it up
keep it up
gor blimey.'

man, 46, and mother-in-law
London

Tune: 'I should be so lucky'

I should be so lucky
with my rubber ducky
strangle Mrs Mangle too.
Steph'nie had a baby
called it Stupid Jamie
and that's the end of Neighbours too.

girl, 6
London

Tune: 'These Foolish Things'

A sweaty sock beside an old French letter
a dose of syphilis that won't get better
my foreskin stings and all these things
remind me of you.

A pair of testicles with lipstick traces
the night you caught your tits in my new braces
my foreskin stings and all these things
remind me of you.

G. Crawford, 20-ish
Lincoln

121

Tune: 'An English Country Garden'

What do you do
if you want to do a poo?
In an English Country Garden.

Pull down your pants
and suffocate the ants.
In an English Country Garden.

Then get some grass
and wipe it up your arse.
In an English Country Garden.

Then get a leaf
and wipe your underneath.
In an English Country Garden.

Then get a spade
and bury what you made.
In an English Country Garden.

That's what you do
If you want to do a poo,
In an English Country Garden.

girls, 7
London

Tune: 'Kookaburra Sits in the Old Gum Tree'

Kookaburra sitting on the hot tin wire
jumping up and down with his bum on fire.
Scream kookaburra, scream
how hot your arse must be.

Louise Davies-Jones, 17
Bristol

Tune: 'Old Smokey'

On top of old Smokey
all covered in grass,
a bald-headed eagle
sat scratching its . . .

Now don't get mistaken
and don't get misled,
that bald-headed eagle
was scratching its head.

Kate Lawrie, 18, and sister, 19
Bucks

Tune: 'One Man Went To Mow'

One man went to mow,
went to mow a meadow;
one man went to mow,
went to mow a meadow;
one man went to mow,
went to mow a meadow;
one man and his dog, Spot,
a bottle of pop
sausage roll
pink ice-cream
change at Bank for Golders Green
Old Mother Riley and her cow
to milk it, to milk it,
she didn't know how,
she pulled its tail
instead of its tit
and all she got
was a bucketful of shit
went to mow a meadow.

man, 42
Middlesex

Tune: 'Oh dear what can the matter be?'

Oh dear what can the matter be?
Three old ladies stuck in the lavatory,
they've been there from Monday to Saturday
nobody knew they were there.

The first was called Elizabeth Porter
went there to get rid of some unwanted water.
The second was called Elizabeth Humphrey
who sat on the lav and couldn't get her bum free.
The third was called Elizabeth List
went in with a bottle and came out pissed.

Katie, 12
Clwyd

Tune: 'The Old Grey Mare'

The old black bull said,
'Let's have anothery
down by the shrubbery,
you bring the rubbery.'

The old brown cow said,
'You can go to buggery
I ain't gonna do it no more.'

John, 28, and Linda, 25, Motyka
Melbourne, Australia

Tune: 'My Old Man's a Dustman'

My old man's a dustman
he wears a dustman's hat
he took me round the corner
to watch a football match.

Fatty passed to Skinny,
Skinny passed it back.
Fatty took a rotten shot
and knocked the goalie flat.

Where was the goalie
when the ball was in the net?
Half-way round the goal post
with his knickers round his neck.

They put him on a stretcher
they put him on a bed
along came a little dog
and piddled on his head.

Kirsty Sloman, 19, and Russell Couper, 19
Cornwall

If you go down to the woods today
you're sure to have a surprise.
If you go down to the woods today
you'll never believe your eyes,
because mum and dad are having a shag,
Uncle Frank is having a wank
and Auntie D is having it off with grandad.

girl, 9
London

Tune: 'Jesus Christ Superstar'

Jesus Christ, Superstar!
Come down to earth on a Yamaha.
Done a skid,
killed a kid,
and mashed his balls
on a dustbin lid.

boy, 11
London

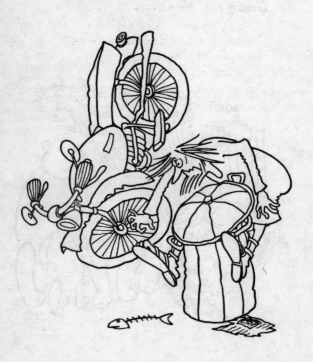

Sung

Everybody's doing it, doing it, doing it,
Picking their nose and chewing it, chewing it.

man, 42
Middlesex

Tune: 'Ten Green Bottles'

Ten black widows hanging on a wall.
Ten black widows hanging on a wall,
and if one black widow
should accidentally fall,
she will climb up his trousers
and paralyse his balls.

boy, 8
London

Ta-ra-ra Boom-de-ay!
My knickers flew away,
I found them on a motorway.

girl, 12
London

Tune: 'Sam Hall'

His name was Knobbly Hall, Knobbly Hall;
His name was Knobbly Hall, Knobbly Hall;
His name was Knobbly Hall
and he only had one ball.
His name was Knobbly Hall, Knobbly Hall.

He went to rob a bank, rob a bank;
He went to rob a bank, rob a bank;
He went to rob a bank
on the way he had a wank.
He went to rob a bank, rob a bank.

The policeman caught him quick, caught him quick;
The policeman caught him quick, caught him quick;
The policeman caught him quick
and hung him by his dick.
The policeman caught him quick, caught him quick.

The judge's name was Hunt, his name was Hunt;
The judge's name was Hunt, his name was Hunt;
The judge's name was Hunt
he was a silly cunt.
The judge's name was Hunt, his name was Hunt.

They hung poor Knobbly Hall, Knobbly Hall;
They hung poor Knobbly Hall, Knobbly Hall;
They hung poor Knobbly Hall
by his last remaining ball.
They hung poor Knobbly Hall, Knobbly Hall.

They buried him in a pit, in a pit;
They buried him in a pit, in a pit;
They buried him in a pit
that pit was full of shit.
They buried him in a pit, in a pit.

girl, 10
London

Tune: 'Colonel Bogey'

Hitler
has only got one ball
Goering
has two but very small
Himmler
is very sim'lar
and poor old Goebbels
has no balls at all.

man, 43
Middlesex

Hitler has only got one ball.
The other is in the county hall.
His mother, the dirty bugger,
Cut it off, when he was small.

boy, 11
London

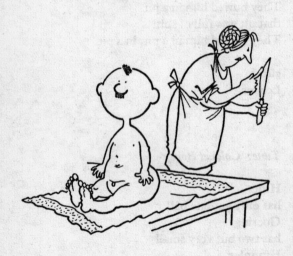

Sung

Rudolph the red-nosed reindeer
had a very shiny cock
and if you ever touched it
you'd get an electric shock.

girl, 10
London

Tune: 'Villikins and Dinah'

As Rachel was walking in the garden one day,
'Sei geschwind, sei geschwind', her mother did say.
'Go and put on your best shabbes clothes
Chaim schmerel is waiting with the big grobbe nose.'

'sei geschwind' = be quick
'shabbes' = sabbath
'Chaim' is a name (James)
'schmerel' = fool
'grobbe' = horrible, gross

man, 68
London

My old man's a dustman
he wears a dustman's hat.
He farted through the keyhole
and paralysed the cat.
The chairs couldn't take it,
the table split in half
that's when my dad
done a supersonic fart.

girl, 11
London

Tune: 'Captain Pugwash'

Do your balls hang low?
Can you swing 'em to and fro?
Can you tie 'em in a knot?
Can you tie 'em in a bow?
Do you get a funny feeling
when your bollocks hit the ceiling?
Oh you'll never be a sailor
if your balls hang low.

Miss G. K. Crawford
Lincoln

Tune: 'I've been everywhere, man'

I was sitting in the corner
of a dirty greasy spoon cafe.
I was putting on the relish
when the man beside me came to say,
'What's that pubic hair doin'
sittin' layin' on yer bins?'
I said I didn't see it there,
could it really be the one?
He jumped upon the counter
and he said, 'Hey looky here
ah bin all over the country
an' ah seen pubic hair.

Ah seen pubic hair, man
more than ah kin bear, man,
even got my share, man
beneath mah underwear, man
ah seen pubic hair, man.'

Sheila, 17
Hampstead, London

136

Tune: 'Daisy Daisy'

Daisy, Daisy
give me your tits to chew.
I'm half crazy
my bollocks are turning blue.
I can't afford a Durex
a plastic bag will do.
but you'll look sweet
upon the seat,
with me on top of you.

Kate Angel, 21
London
(slightly different version) Julian Foster, 18
Beckenham, Kent

Tune: 'Puff the Magic Dragon'

Puff the magic dragon,
pissed in the sea
so they rubbed his bum
in boiling rum
for doing this, you see.

man, 32
Johannesburg, South Africa

Tune: 'Jailhouse Rock'

I went to a party down the county jail
I caught my cock on a rusty nail.
When I got home I was in for a shock:
I only had one ball on my cock.

I've been invited to a nudist colony,
I won't go, oh deary, deary me
because they'll be laughing at my dapper
saying I look like Adolf Hitler.

Nick the Greek, 26
London

Tune: 'Rule Britannia'

Rule Britannia
two tanners make a bob.
Good King Henry
never shaved his knob.

Richard Griffiths, 25
Beeston, Notts

Tune: 'Red Flag'

The working class can kiss my arse
I've got the foreman's job at last.
If you're out of work and on the dole,
you can stick the Red Flag up your hole.

John Bolt
Stroud, Gloucs

Tune: 'My Bonnie Lies Over the Ocean'

My daddy lies over the ocean
my mummy lies over the sea.
My daddy laid over my mummy
and that's how they got little me.

children, 10
Kensington, London

Tune: 'Stand Up Stand Up For Jesus'

Sit down
sit down
for Christ's sake,
the buggers at the back can't see.

man, 69
London

Sung

I don't care if it snows or freezes,
I am Jesus' little lamb.
I am safe in the arms of Jesus
Yes, by Jesus Christ, I am.

man, 68
London

Sung

Good King Wenceslas looked out
upon his cabbage garden.
He farted on a Brussels sprout
and said, I beg your pardon.

girl, 8
Surrey

Tune: 'My Little Pony'

My little pony
skinny and bony
born in a stable
drinking Black Label
that stupid swine
cost 5.99

Abigail Kristy Silvester, 12
London

Tune: Signature tune for 'Rainbow'

Flying up above streets and houses
Bungle's flying high,
opens up his hairy arse
and shits in Jeffrey's eye.

boy, 7
London

'Rainbow'

In the jungle
Zippy and Bungle
having lots of fun;
Zippy got silly
and pulled out his willy
and shoved it up Bungle's bum.

boys, 12
London

Tune: 'The Snowman' [as in film]

We're walking through the air,
I've lost my underwear
I'm going to Mothercare
to buy
another pair
to wear . . .

boy, 8
London

Sung

I'm Popeye the sailor man,
I live in a caravan.
There's a hole in the middle
where I do my piddle.
I'm Popeye the sailor man,
poop, poop.

I'm Popeye the sailor man,
I live in a frying pan.
Turn up the gas
burn up my ass.
I'm Popeye the sailor man,
poop, poop.

I'm Popeye the sailor man,
I live in a caravan.
When I go swimming
I kiss all the women.
I'm Popeye the sailor man,
poop, poop.

I'm Popeye the sailor man,
I live in a pot of jam.
And it's so sticky
it sticks to my dicky.
I'm Popeye the sailor man,
poop, poop.

boys, 8 and 11
London

Needing to go to the Loo by Ivor Poo, Willie Makeit, Betty Wont

Andrew Drury, 13
Derby

Wanking by Paul Backskin

boy, 14
London

Bubbles in the Bath by Ivor Wynn D. Bottom

boy, 17, and girl, 13, Surrey
man, 53, Calgary, Canada

The Cat's Revenge by Claud Balls

man, 53
Calgary, Canada

Run to the Toilet by Willie Makeit

John, 28, and Linda, 25, Motyka
Melbourne, Australia

Nail on the Banister by R. Stornaway

Piddle on the Bathroom Floor by I. P. Squint

Anne, 40; Eileen, 42; Jean, 30
Edinburgh

Yellow River by I. P. Daily

Baby's Revenge by Nora Titoff

John, 28, and Linda, 25, Motyka
Melbourne, Australia

Rusty Bedsprings by I. P. Knightly

Twenty Years in the Saddle by Major Bumsore

Dirty Walls by Hoo Flung Dung

1 girl, 13
London
2, 3 man, 42
London

There was a young fellow from Brent
whose knob was unusually bent.
So to save him the trouble,
he put it in double
and instead of coming, he went.

man, 46
London

A clever commercial female
had prices tattooed to her tail.
And below her behind
for the sake of the blind
a duplicate version in braille.

Petra Hooks, 14
Reading

There was a young man from St Paul's
who possessed the most useless of balls.
One night in the Strand
he managed to stand
and tossed himself off in the stalls.

Lee Dawson Geldard, 14
Bridlington, North Humberside

There was a young actress from Kew
who said, as the bishop withdrew,
'The vicar is quicker,
and slicker and thicker,
and three inches longer than you.'

Michael Sharp Jnr, 16
Leeds

There was a young plumber named Lee
who plumbed his girl down by the sea.
Said the lady, 'Stop plumbing,
I hear someone coming.'
Said the plumber, still plumbing, 'That's me!'

Carla Holden, 15
Cumbria

There was an old man from Boshum
who took out his balls to wash 'em.
Then his wife said, 'Jack,
if you don't put 'em back
I will stamp on the fuckers and squash 'em.'

Eileen McLarnon, 14, Grantham, Lincs
girl, 11, London

There was a young woman called Ransom
who was fucked nine times in a hansom.
When she called out for more,
the man on the floor
said, 'My name's Simpson, not Samson.'

man, 46
London

The first mate's name was Carter
and boy! was he a farter
when the wind was low
and the ship wouldn't go
they used Carter the Farter to start'er.

John, 28, and Linda, 25, Motyka
Melbourne, Australia

There was a young man called Perkins
who took a fond liking to gherkins.
One day on a spree
he ate two-forty-three
and fucked up his internal workings.

Nick the Greek, 26
London

There was an old man called Denzil
whose prick was as sharp as a pencil.
It went through an actress,
three sheets and a mattress
and shattered a bedroom utensil.

man, 42
Middlesex

There was an old man called Jock
who had a fifty foot cock.
It hit a tree
and he pissed on a flea
and twisted it round a rock.

Terence Chambers, 13
Lincs

There once was a man from Brazil
who took an atomic pill.
His legs expired
his bum backfired
and his cock shot over the hill.

girl, 16
North Island, New Zealand

There was a young woman named Sally
who stripped at the working men's Palais
she got lots of applause
when she pulled down her drawers
'cos the hairs on her head didn't tally.

Barry Saunders, 31
Herts

There was a young hooker from Crewe
who filled her vagina with glue.
She said with a grin
'If they pay to get in
they can pay to get out again too.'

Miss Debra Wride, 23
Birmingham

There was an old man from Guyana
who learnt how to play the piano.
His fingers slipped
and his fly buttons ripped
and out popped a hairy banana.

man, 42
Middlesex

There once was a man called Green
who invented a wanking machine.
His wife, she awoke
the fucking thing broke
and whipped his balls to cream.

Phil Goodwin, 26
Doncaster

There was an old man from Crocket
who went to the moon in a rocket.
The rocket went bang,
his balls went clang,
and his dick ended up in his pocket.

D. Pritchard, 31
learnt at 9
Accrington, Lancs

There once was a man called Reg
who got off with a girl in the hedge.
Along came his wife
with a carving knife,
and cut off his meat and two veg.

Kate Rosewell, 11
Bridgehampton, Somerset

There was a young man from Rangoon
who was born three months too soon.
He hadn't the luck
to be born with a fuck
He was scraped off the bed with a spoon.

Mrs F. Longson, 88
Derbyshire

You start as somebody's sperms
end, being eaten by worms.
And the part in between
is, as you've seen
full of diseases and germs.

Terry Cuthbert, 43
Oxford

The height of agony:
sliding down a razor blade
using your knob as a brake.

A cad:
someone who goes round a johnny factory
with a pin
putting holes in all the johnny bags.

Height of luxury:
fur-lined johnny
with a zip fastener.

Height of impossibility:
a flea wiping an elephant's arse
with a piece of confetti.

man, 42
Middlesex

Success:
Two gays walking down the street with a pram.

Pain:
Sliding down a razor blade using your balls as stoppers.

girl, 13
Bucks

A bra:
Over the shoulder boulder holder
Upper decker flopper stopper.

A jock strap:
Lower decker knacker jacket.

Mrs Holmes, from 1970s
Fareham, Hants

Innocence:
Nuns doing press-ups in a cucumber field.

Russell Wernham, 16
Berks

Agony:
Horse in a wet suit having an erection.

Frustration:
One-armed bandit hanging off a cliff with itchy balls.

Louise Davies-Jones, 17, Bristol
Andrew Drury, 13, Derby

A bum:
Kojak with a splitting headache.

boy, 9
London

Impossibility:
trying to pin diarrhoea to the wall.

Kate Lawrie, 18, and sister, 19
Bucks

A prostitute is like a police station:
Dicks going in and out.

D. R. Freeman, 41
Surrey

A drawing pin:
A Smartie with an erection.

A snail:
A bogy with a crash helmet.

girl, 11
Brill, Bucks

The angle
of the dangle
is directly proportional
to the height of the shelf
the magazine came from.

boy, 15
Strathclyde

The angle of the dangle
is proportional to the sag of the bag
as long as the heat of the meat
remains constant.

man, 44
Hertfordshire

A potato is a potato
a tomato is a tomato
and a pea is a relief.

Karen Godliman, 13
Woking, Surrey

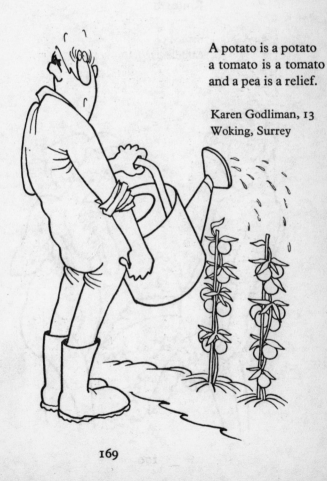

Stiff and straight
long and thin
all wrapped up
in a shiny pink skin.

What is it?

Rhubarb

man, 43
Middlesex

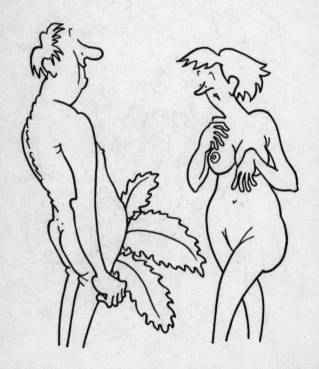

How do you tell a Scotman's clan?

Put your hand up his kilt and if he's got a
Quarterpounder
he's a Macdonald.

Chris Mangnall, 14
Lancashire

What are three bad things about being a dick?
1. Your two best mates are nuts and an arsehole.
2. Your master covers you with a plastic bag.
3. Every time you get excited, you throw up.

Jack Staples, 13
South London

What's pink and hangs out your boxer shorts?

Your mum on washing day.

boy, 15
Strathclyde

I thought it'd be all right . . .

You know what Thought did, don't you? Followed a dung cart 'cos he thought it was a wedding; piddled in his pants 'cos he thought they weren't there . . .

man, 44
London

Riddle

My Auntie Mary
has a thing hairy.
My Uncle John
has a thing long.
My Uncle John
put his thing long
into Auntie Mary's hairy.

What is it?
Broom handle and broom.

Dr Tim Healey, 55
Barnsley

How is sex like maths?

Subtract clothes
add bed
divide legs
and multiply.

boy, 15
Strathclyde

Georgie Porgie pudding and pie
kissed the girls and made them cry.
When the boys came out to play
he kissed them too – he's funny that way.

Georgie (!), 5
Hammersmith

Goosey Goosey Gander
where do you wander?
Upstairs and downstairs
and in my lady's chamber.
There I saw an old man
playing with his dick.
So I took him by the left leg
and gave his arse a kick.

policeman, 40
Ealing, Middlesex

Sung

I'm a little tea-pot
short and silly.
Here's my handle
here's my willy.
When the tea is ready
hear me hiss.
Lift me up
and see me piss.

man, 44
London

Old Mother Hubbard
went to the cupboard
to fetch poor Rover a bone
when she bent over
Rover took over
and gave her a bone of his own.

Reg Palmer, 20, Middlesex
Richard Dod, 13, S. Wirral

Old Mother Hubbard went to the cupboard
to fetch the postman a letter.
When she got there
the cupboard was bare
so they had it without – it was better.

Jonathan Nash, 21
Derbyshire

Wee Willie Winkie runs through the town
with his knickers hanging down.

boy, 11
Northern Ireland

Matthew Mark Luke and John
went to bed with their trousers on.
Luke woke up in the middle of the night
and said he had to do a shite.

Now a shite is a thing that must be done,
so out of the window he popped his bum.
PC Parker on his midnight beat
mistook his arse for a burglar's feet.
'Come down, you rascal,' the copper did cry.
Wallop, dollop, shit fell in his eye.

man, 68
London

Little Miss Muffet sat on a tuffet
her knickers all tattered and torn.
It wasn't the spider that sat down beside 'er;
It was Little Boy Blue with the horn.

girl, 14
London

Oh the Grand Old Duke of York
he had ten thousand men.
(And his court case comes up tomorrow.)

Paul Stanfield, 22
Stoke-on-Trent

Hey fiddle fiddle
the cat done a piddle
all over the bathroom mat.
The little dog laughed
to see such fun
so he peed all over the cat.

Hey fiddle fiddle
the dog done a piddle
all over the kitchen floor.
The little dog laughed
to see such fun
so he done a little bit more.

girl, 13
London

Jack and Jill went up the hill
to do some hanky-panky.
Jack went, 'Ooh,'
Jill went, 'Ahh,'
then out popped Baby Frankie.

Karen Godliman, 13
Woking, Surrey

Jack and Jill went to the dairy
Jack pulled out his big and hairy.
Jill said, 'Oh what a whopper,
let's get down and do it proper.'

girl, 11, London
Richard Griffiths, 25
Beeston, Notts
Jamie Jones, 12
Manchester
Mark Poole, 15
East Yorkshire

Jack and Jill went up the hill
to fetch a pail of water.
I don't know what they did up there
but they came down with a daughter.

Jack and Jill went up the hill
to fetch a pail of water.
I don't know what they did up there
but I know they never oughta.

boys, 12
London

Tune: 'Half a pound of Tuppenny Rice'

Half a pound of Mandy Rice
half a pound of Keeler,
neither girl is very nice,
everybody feel her.

Dr Tim Healey, 55
Barnsley

Jack be nimble
Jack be quick
Jack jump over the candlestick;
silly boy
should have jumped higher
goodness gracious!
Great balls of fire!

boy, 16
Cairo, Egypt

Old King Cole
was a merry old soul
and a merry old soul was he.
He called for a light
in the middle of the night
to go to the lavatory.
The moon shone bright
on the shit-house door;
the candle had a fit.
Old King Cole
fell down the hole
and came out covered in shit.

girl, 13
London

Mistress Mary,
quite contrary,
how hairy
is your canary?
Three or four
inches long?
Or are you a toff
and shave them off?

Nick the Greek, 26
London

There was an old woman
who lived in a bucket.
I had a good rhyme,
but Mum made me chuck it.

Dr Tim Healey, 55
Barnsley

There was an old lady
who lived in a shoe,
she had no children
she knew what to do.

Dr Tim Healey, 55
Barnsley

Mary had a little lamb
she kept it as a pet.
And when the price of meat went up,
she ate the little get.

Mary had a little lamb
she fed it on crackers.
Every time it jumped the fence
it landed on its knackers.

Lee Dawson Geldard, 14
Bridlington, North Humberside

Mary had a little lamb
the butcher chopped it dead,
she took it to school the next day
between two hunks of bread.

John Bolt
Stroud, Gloucs

Mary had a little lamb
she kept it in a bucket
and every time the lamb jumped out,
the bulldog tried to put it back again.

John Bolt
Stroud, Gloucs

Mary had a little lamb
and a little duck,
she put them on the mantelpiece
to see if they would fall off.

man, 42
Middlesex

Mary had a little lamb
she thought it very silly,
she threw it up into the air
and caught it by its willy
was a bulldog sitting on the grass,
along came a bumble-bee
and stung him on the
ask no questions,
tell no lies,
I never seen a copper
doing up his flies
are a nuisance,
bees are worse.
That's the end
of my silly verse.

girl, 13
London

Mary had a little lamb . . .
. . . she got 2 years for perverting a minor
and 10 for bestiality.

boy, 17
near Godalming

Mary had a little lamb
it was white as snow.
She put it on the mantelpiece
and it piddled in granma's cocoa.

Kerry Connor, 11
Sennelager, Germany

Mary had a little watch
she used it as a garter
when the boys asked the time
she knew what they were after.

Danny, 36
Bromley, Kent

Mary had a little lamb,
she tied it to a pylon.
10,000 volts went up its arse,
and turned its wool to nylon.

Lee Dawson Geldard, 14, Bridlington, North Humberside
Karen Godliman, 13, Woking, Surrey
Jamie Jones, 12, Manchester
Eileen McLarnon, 14, Lincs

Mary had a little sheep
With her one night, it went to sleep.
The sheep turned out to be a ram,
now Mary has a little lamb.

playground (4-year-olds)
Hammersmith, 1989

Mary had a little lamb
the doctor was surprised
but when Macdonald had a farm
he couldn't believe his eyes.

Richard Griffiths, 25
Beeston, Notts

A Load of Walls

Sign in a railway station

Toilets out of order,
please use platforms 5 and 6.

boy, 17, and girl, 13
Surrey

On the door of 'The Wee Room'

We aim to please,
You aim, too, please.

girl, 13
London

Notice Seen on a Director's Door

Never before in the whole of my life
have I ever met anyone with as many problems
and such bad luck as you have.
Your story has really touched my heart –
now piss off and stop bothering me.

Jonathan Nash, 21
Derbyshire

When things go wrong
and they usually will
and your daily road
seems all uphill
when machines are down
and tempers high
when you try to smile
but can only cry
and you really feel
you'd like to quit,
don't run to me,
I don't give a shit.

Tim Isaacs, 14
Cambridge

Here I sit as bored as hell
waiting for the fucking bell.

Kate Lawrie, 18, and sister, 19
Bucks

Note left by bride, pinned to pillow

The shoehorn's on the mantelpiece
the Vaseline's on the shelf.
I saw that great big thing of yours,
so I chloroformed myself.

Dr Tim Healey, 55
Barnsley

Written on a Toilet Wall

If you sprinkle
while you twinkle
be discreet
and wipe the seat.

Petra Hooks, 14
Reading

To all who use these marble halls,
use the paper
not the walls.

mother-in-law
London

Don't throw your fag ends in the loo
you know it isn't right.
It makes them very soggy
and impossible to light.

boy, 17, and girl, 13
Surrey

It's no use standing on the seat,
the crabs in here can jump six feet.

Dr Tim Healey, 55
Barnsley

If in this bog there is no paper
under the seat you'll find a scraper.
If the scraper cannot be found
drag your arse across the ground.

Chris Mangnall, 14
Lancashire

Here I sit broken hearted
paid my penny
and only farted.

man, 42
Middlesex